CW00386391

Red Peppers

AN INTERLUDE WITH MUSIC FROM
Tonight at 8:30

By Noel Coward

SAMUEL FRENCH, INC.
45 West 25th Street   NEW YORK 10001
7623 Sunset Boulevard HOLLYWOOD 90046
LONDON   TORONTO

RED PEPPERS

Produced by John C. Wilson at the National Theatre in New York City on November 24, 1936, as one of a series of nine one-act plays by Noel Coward, under the title of "TO-NIGHT AT EIGHT-THIRTY." The play was directed by the author and the cast was as follows:

GEORGE PEPPER	*Noel Coward.*
LILY PEPPER	*Gertrude Lawrence.*
BERT BENTLEY	*Anthony Pelissier.*
MR. EDWARDS	*Alan Webb.*
MABEL GRACE	*Joyce Carey.*
ALF	*Kenneth Carten.*

The action of the play takes place on the stage, a dressing-room, and the stage again of the Palace of Varieties in one of the smaller English provincial towns.

The time is Saturday night, present day.

Sheet music, two songs, available $1.25 each, plus postage

RED PEPPERS

First produced at the Opera House, Manchester, and subsequently at the Phœnix Theatre, Charing Cross Road, London, W.C.2, in January, 1936, with the following cast of characters :

GEORGE PEPPER	*Noel Coward.*
LILY PEPPER	*Gertrude Lawrence.*
BERT BENTLEY	*Anthony Pelissier.*
MR. EDWARDS	*Alan Webb.*
MABEL GRACE	*Alison Leggatt.*
ALF	*Kenneth Carten.*

The action of the play takes place on the stage, a dressing-room, and the stage again of the Palace of Varieties in one of the smaller English provincial towns.

The time is Saturday night, present day.

RED PEPPERS

The interlude occurs in The Palace Theatre of Varieties in one of the smaller English provincial towns on a Saturday night.

GEORGE *and* LILY PEPPER *are a singing and dancing comedy act. They are both somewhere in the thirties. They have been married for many years and in the Profession since they were children. Their act consists of a " Man About Town " Dude number, for which they wear smooth red wigs, tails, silk hats and canes, and a " Sailor " number, for which they wear curly red wigs, sailor clothes with exaggerated bell-bottomed trousers and carry telescopes.*

GEORGE *and* LILY *have just finished one number before a front cloth street scene.*

GEORGE. If you will allow my wife and I time to change our costumes, we will give you our famous nautical extravaganza.—Thank you, Bert. (*He runs off to* R.)

(*The orchestra plays one blaring refrain of their sailor number, at the end of which they enter doing a sailor's roll with their telescopes under their arms. In the middle of the rumber they do their patter, which consists of a series of well-worn quick-fire gags, then they do one more refrain, a soi-disant hornpipe and their exit, in course of which* LILY *drops her telescope.*)

SAILOR NUMBER : " HAS ANYBODY SEEN OUR SHIP ! "

Verse 1.

BOTH. What shall we do with the drunken sailor !
So the saying goes.
We're not tight but we're none too bright,
Great Scott ! I don't suppose !

7

We've lost our way
And we've lost our pay,
And to make the thing complete
We've been and gone and lost the bloomin' fleet!

Refrain 1.

Has anybody seen our ship,
The H.M.S. " Peculiar " ?
We've been on shore
For a month or more,
And when we see the Captain we shall get
    " what for."
Heave ho, me hearties,
Sing Glory Halleluiah.
A lady bold as she could be
Pinched our whistles at " The Golden Key,"
Now we're in between the devil and the deep
    blue sea !
Has anybody seen our ship ?

(*Ad lib. from the orchestra.*)

LILY. Here, George ! Who was that lady I saw you walking down the street with the other morning ?

GEORGE. That wasn't a lady, that was my wife !

LILY. Keep it clean. Keep it fresh. Keep it fragrant !

GEORGE. Was that your little dog I saw you with in the High Street ?

LILY. Yes, that was my little dog.

GEORGE. What's his name ?

LILY. Fruit Salts.

GEORGE. Fruit Salts ?

LILY. Yes, Fruit Salts.

GEORGE. Why ?

LILY. Ask him—Eno's !

GEORGE. Keep it clean. Keep it fresh. Keep it fragrant ! (*To* VIOLINIST.) It'll never get well if you pick it. (*To* LILY.) Why did you leave school ?

LILY. Appendicitis.

GEORGE. Appendicitis ?

LILY. Yes, appendicitis.

GEORGE. What do you mean—appendicitis ?

LILY. Couldn't spell it !

GEORGE. I heard you had adenoids.

LILY. Adenoids ?

GEORGE. Yes, adenoids.

LILY. Don't speak of it.

GEORGE. Why not ?

LILY. Adenoids me !

BOTH. La la la la—la la la la !

GEORGE. I saw a very strange thing the other day.

LILY. What was it ?

GEORGE. Twelve men standing under one umbrella and they didn't get wet.

LILY. How's that ?

GEORGE. It wasn't raining !

LILY. Do you know what a skeleton is ?

GEORGE. Do I know what a skeleton is ?

LILY. Do you know what a skeleton is ?

GEORGE. Yes.

LILY. Well, what is it ?

GEORGE. A lot of bones with the people scraped off !

LILY. Keep it clean. Keep it fresh. Keep it fragrant!

GEORGE. Why is getting up at six o'clock in the morning like a pig's tail ?

LILY. I don't know, George. Why is getting up at six o'clock in the morning like a pig's tail ?

GEORGE. Twirly.

LILY. Where did you go last night ?

GEORGE. The cemetery.

LILY. Anyone dead ?

GEORGE. All of 'em !

Refrain 2.

BOTH. Has anybody seen our ship,
The H.M.S. " Disgusting " ?
We've three guns aft
And another one fore,
And they've promised us a funnel for the
next world war.

Heave ho, me hearties,
The quarter-deck needs dusting.
We had a binge last Christmas year,
Nice plum pudding and a round of beer,
But the Captain pulled his cracker and we
      cried, " Oh, dear !
Has anybody seen our ship ? "

Refrain 3.

Has anybody seen our ship,
The H.M.S. " Suggestive " ?
She sailed away
Across the bay,
And we haven't had a smell of her since New
      Year's Day.
Heave ho, me hearties,
We're getting rather restive.
We pooled our money, spent the lot,
The world forgetting, by the world forgot,
Now we haven't got a penny for the you know
      what !
Has anybody seen our ship ?

Verse 2.   (*If necessary.*)

What's to be done with the girls on shore
Who lead our Tars astray ?
What's to be done with the drinks galore
That make them pass away ?
We got wet ears
From our first five beers,
After that we lost control,
And now we find we're up the blinking pole !

(*Their exit consists of a neat walk off together, one behind
the other, with their telescopes under their arms. Unfor-
tunately, in course of this snappy finale, LILY, who is
behind GEORGE, drops her telescope and hurriedly
retrieves it, thereby ruining the whole effect. GEORGE
shoots her a look of fury and mutters something to her
out of the corner of his mouth. The CURTAIN falls and*

*they take a call before it, breathless and smiling, but
with a certain quality of foreboding behind their smiles.)*

The CURTAIN *rises on the interior of their dressing-room.
It is a fairly squalid room, for although they are com-
paratively well known in the provinces, they have never,
to date, achieved the dignity of the star dressing-room
or the pride of topping the bill. The room is three sides
of a square. Down stage on the* R. *there is a door
leading to the passage. Up stage* C. *there is a lavatory
basin. Up* R. *and up* L. *are wooden hanging arrange-
ments for clothes.*

  GEORGE'S *dressing-place is on the right, and* LILY'S
is on the left.

  (See Photograph of Scene.)

As the CURTAIN *rises on the scene they both enter in silence,
but wearing expressions of set rage. They are still
breathless and extremely hot.* GEORGE *goes to his
dressing-place and* LILY *goes to hers. They both take
off their wigs and fling them down, then, still in silence,
they proceed to rip off their sailor clothes. These are
made with zippers in order to facilitate their quick
change.* LILY *is wearing a brassière and silk knickers,
and* GEORGE *a vest and drawers. They both have black
shoes with taps on them and black socks and sock
suspenders.*

  GEORGE (R.). Now then. *(He sits.)*

  LILY *(putting on her dressing-gown,* L.). Now then
what ?

  GEORGE *(contemptuously).* Now then what !

  LILY. I don't know what you're talking about.
(She sits.)

  GEORGE. Oh, you don't, don't you ?

  LILY. No, I don't, so shut up.

  GEORGE. I suppose you don't know you mucked up
the whole exit !

  LILY. It wasn't my fault.

  GEORGE. Whose fault was it then—Mussolini's !

  LILY *(with sarcasm).* I see. Funny, hey !

GEORGE (*witheringly*). I suppose you didn't drop your prop, did you ? And having dropped it, you didn't have to go back for it, leaving me to prance off all by meself—who d'you think you are, Rebla ?

LILY. Never mind about that—the exit was too quick.

GEORGE. It was the same as it's always been.

LILY. It was too quick, I tell you, it's been too quick the whole week ; the whole number's too quick——

GEORGE. Bert Bentley takes that number at the same tempo as he's always done.

LILY. You and your Bert Bentley. Just because he stands you a Welsh rarebit at the Queen's you think he's God Almighty.

GEORGE. Bert Bentley's the best conductor in the North of England and don't you make any mistake about it.

LILY. Best conductor my foot ! I suppose he thinks it's funny to see us leaping up and down the stage like a couple of greyhounds.

GEORGE. If you're a greyhound, I'm Fred Astaire.

LILY. Oh, you're Fred Astaire all right, with a bit of Pavlova thrown in—you're wonderful, you are—there's nothing you can't do, except behave like a gentleman.

GEORGE. Oh, so you expect me to behave like a gentleman, do you ? That's a good one, coming from you.

LILY. Oh, shut up, you make me tired.

GEORGE. I make *you* tired ! I suppose it was me that mucked up the exit—I suppose it was me that dropped me bloody telescope !

LILY (*heated—rises and crosses* C.). Now look here, George Pepper——

GEORGE (*rises and crosses* C.). Stop George Peppering me—why can't you admit it when you're in the wrong ?—You mucked up the exit—nobody else did—you did !

LILY. Well, what if I did ? It was an accident, wasn't it ? I didn't do it on purpose.

GEORGE. It doesn't matter how you did it or why you did it—you did it.

LILY (*screaming*). All right, I did it!

GEORGE (*triumphantly*). Well, don't do it again.

(*There is a knock on the door.*)

LILY. Who is it?

ALF (*outside*). Me. Alf.

LILY. All right, come in.

(ALF, *the callboy, enters. He is laden with the* PEPPERS' *discarded evening suits, silk hats and canes. He plumps them down.*)

ALF. There.

GEORGE. Thanks. (*He gets some money out of his coat pocket.*) Here, tell Fred to pop out and get me twenty Player's and a large Guinness.

LILY (*taking her clothes*). Why can't you wait and have it with your steak?

GEORGE. You mind yours and I'll mind mine.

ALF. You'll have to wait until Mabel Grace is finished.

LILY (*taking his clothes*). She's been finished for years as far as I'm concerned.

GEORGE. What's the matter with Mabel Grace?

LILY. Ask the public, dear; just ask the public.

ALF (*about to leave*). Same as usual, I suppose, between the houses?

GEORGE. Yes, and tell 'em not to forget the salt, like they did last night.

ALF. Righto.

(ALF *goes out.*)

(LILY *starts to pack various things into a large hamper which has emblazoned on it in large black letters :* " *The Red Peppers.*")

GEORGE. What did you want to say that about Mabel Grace for in front of him?

LILY (*grandly*). It happens to be my opinion.

GEORGE. Well, in future you'd better keep your opinions to yourself in front of strangers.

LILY (*mumbling*). If you're so fond of Mabel Grace I wonder you don't go and ask her for her autograph—she'd drop dead if you did. (*She goes to the basin to wash.*)

GEORGE. Mabel Grace is an artist and don't you forget it—she may be a bit long in the tooth now, but she's a bigger star than you'll ever be, so there !

LILY (*crossing* L. *for a towel*). You make me sick, sucking up to the top-liners.

GEORGE (*washing at the basin up* C.). Who sucks up to the top-liners ?

LILY. You do—look at Irene Baker !

GEORGE. What's the matter with Irene Baker ?

LILY. When last heard from she was falling down drunk at the Empire, Hartlepool.

GEORGE (*coming to her*). That's a dirty lie : Irene never touches a drop till after the show, and well you know it.

LILY (*contemptuously*). Irene ! It was Miss Baker this and Miss Baker that, the last time you saw her.

GEORGE. That's all you know. (*He crosses* R. *above the basket.*)

LILY. Trying to make me think you got off with her, eh ? What a chance !

GEORGE. Oh, shut up nagging !

LILY (*muttering*). Irene——!

GEORGE. If a day ever dawns when you can time your laughs like Irene Baker does, I'll give you a nice red apple !

LILY. Time my laughs ! That's funny. Fat lot of laughs I get when you write the gags.

GEORGE (*grandly*). If you're dissatisfied with your material you know what you can do with it. (*Putting on his dressing-gown.*)

LILY. I know what I'd like to do with it.

GEORGE. You can't even do a straight walk off without balling it up.

LILY. Oh, we're back at that again, are we ?

GEORGE (C.). Yes, we are, so there!

LILY (*moving over to him*). Now look here, just you listen to me for a minute. . . .

GEORGE. I've been listening to you for fifteen years, one more minute won't hurt.

LILY. I've had about enough of this. I'm sick of you and the whole act. It's lousy, anyway.

GEORGE (*sits* R.). The act was good enough for my Mum and Dad and it's good enough for you.

LILY (*with heavy sarcasm*). Times have changed a bit since your Mum and Dad's day, you know. There's electric light now and telephones and a little invention called Moving Pictures. Nobody wants to see the Red Peppers for three bob when they can see Garbo for ninepence! (*She sits* L., *brushing her hat.*)

GEORGE. That's just where you're wrong, see! We're flesh and blood, we are—the public would rather see flesh and blood any day than a cheesy photograph. Put Garbo on on a Saturday night in Devonport and see what would happen to her!

LILY. Yes, look what happened to us!

GEORGE. That wasn't Devonport, it was Southsea.

LILY. Well, wherever it was, the Fleet was in.

GEORGE. If you think the act's so lousy it's a pity you don't re-write some of it.

LILY. Ever tried going into St. Paul's and offering to re-write the Bible?

GEORGE. Very funny! Oh, very funny indeed. You're wasted in the show business, you ought to write for "Comic Cuts," you ought.

LILY. At that I could think up better gags than you do—" That wasn't a lady, that was my wife!" "Why did you leave school? Appendicitis!"—hoary old chestnuts—they were has-beens when your grandmother fell off the high wire.

GEORGE. And what, may I ask, 'as my grandmother got to do with it?

LILY. She didn't fall soon enough, that's all.

GEORGE (*rises and comes over to her—furiously*). You shut your mouth and stop hurling insults at my family.

What were you when I married you, I should like **to** know ! One of the six Moonlight Maids—dainty songs and dances, and no bookings ! (*He crosses back* **R.** *in front of the basket.*)

LILY (*hotly*). When we did get bookings we got number one towns, which is more than your Mum and Dad ever did !

GEORGE. Who wants the number one towns, any-way ? You can't get a public all the year round like my Mum and Dad by doing a parasol dance twice a year at the Hippodrome, Manchester !

LILY. The Moonlight Maids was just as good an act as the Red Peppers any day, and a bloody sight more refined at that !

GEORGE. You've said it. That's just what it was—refined. It was so refined it simpered itself out of the bill—— (*He sits* R.)

LILY. A bit of refinement wouldn't do you any harm——

GEORGE. Perhaps you'd like to change the act to " Musical Moments," with me playing a flute and **you** sitting under a standard lamp with a 'cello ?

(*There is a knock at the door.*)

LILY. Who is it ?
BERT (*outside*). Me—Bert Bentley.
GEORGE. Come in, old man.
LILY (*under her breath*). Old man——

(BERT BENTLEY *enters. He is the musical director, a flashy little man wearing a tail suit and a white waistcoat that is none too clean.*)

BERT (*cheerfully*). Well, well, well, how's tricks ?
GEORGE. Mustn't grumble.
BERT. Anybody got a Gold Flake ?
GEORGE. Here's a Player's, that do ?
BERT (*taking one*). It's your last.
GEORGE. I've sent Fred out for some more. Lucifer !
BERT. Okay—ta.
GEORGE. Sketch on !

BERT. Yes, the old cow's tearing herself to shreds.

GEORGE. It's a pretty strong situation she's got in that sketch—I watched it from the side first house on Wednesday.

BERT. She nearly got the bird second house.

LILY. Too refined, I expect. For this date.

BERT (*crosses to sit on the basket*). Well, they're liable to get a bit restless, you know, when she stabs herself— she takes such an hell of a time about it—that's legits all over—we had Robert Haversham here a couple of months ago—what a make-up—stuck together with stamp paper he was—Robert Haversham the famous tragedian and company ! You should have seen the company : a couple of old tats got up as Elizabethan pages with him doing a death scene in the middle of them—he died all right.

GEORGE. Did he buy it ?

BERT. He bought it—three and eightpence in coppers and a bottle of Kola.

LILY. Poor old man, what a shame.

BERT. Well, what did he want to do it for ? That sort of stuff's no good. They're all alike—a few seasons in the West End and they think they're set.

LILY. Lot of hooligans birding the poor old man.

BERT (*with slight asperity*). This is as good a date as you can get, you know !

LILY. I've played better.

GEORGE. Oh, pipe down, Depression ! (*To* BERT.) Sorry I can't offer you a drink, old man, Fred hasn't brought it yet.

BERT. That's all right, George—I'll have one with you in between the houses. By the way, don't you think that exit of yours is dragging a bit ?

LILY (*explosively*). Dragging !

GEORGE. Lil thinks it was a bit too quick.

BERT. Whatever you say, it's all the same to me.

GEORGE. Maybe you could pep it up a little.

LILY. Maybe it would be better if we did the whole act on skates !

GEORGE (*conciliatively*). Bert's quite right, you know, Lil.

LILY. I don't know any such thing.

BERT. All right, all right, all right—there's no need to get nasty.

GEORGE. Oh, don't take any notice of her, she don't know what she's talking about.

LILY (*with overpowering sweetness*). My husband's quite right, Mr. Bentley, my husband is always quite right. You don't have to pay any attention to me, I don't count—I'm only a feed.

GEORGE. Oh, dry up.

LILY (*continuing—rises, places chair carefully under the table*). But I should just like to say one thing, Mr. Bentley, if you'll forgive me for stepping out of my place for a minute, and that is, that if you take that exit any quicker at the second house, I shall not drop my telescope—— Oh, no—I shall sock you in the chops with it !

BERT (*rises*). Who the hell d'you think you are, talking to me like that !

LILY. You and your orchestra—Orchestra ! More like a hurdy-gurdy and flat at that !

BERT. What's wrong with my orchestra ?

LILY. Nothing, apart from the instruments and the men what play 'em.

BERT. My orchestra's played for the best artists in the business——

LILY (*crosses up to her clothes-rack*). Yes, but not until they were too old to care.

BERT. I didn't come up here to be insulted by a cheap little comedy act.

GEORGE (*incensed*). What's that ! What's that ! What's that !

BERT. You heard. You're damned lucky to get this date at all !

(LILY *crosses L. again.*)

GEORGE. Lucky ! My God, it's a fill in—that's all —a fill in !

BERT. I suppose Nervo and Knox use it as a fill in, and Lily Morris and Flanagan and Allen ?

LILY. They probably have friends living near.

BERT (*making a movement to go*). Before you start saucing me just take a look at your place on the bill—that's all—just take a look at it.

GEORGE. We're in the second half.

BERT. Only because the acrobats can't make their change.

LILY. It's in our contract—after the interval's in our contract.

BERT. Well, make the most of it while you've got it.

GEORGE. Get to hell out of here, you twopenny-halfpenny little squirt—lucky for you we've got another show to play.

BERT. Not so damned lucky—I've got to look at it.

LILY. Well, it'll be the first time—maybe we'll get the tempo right for a change !

BERT. You set your tempos Monday morning and they haven't been changed since.

LILY. That's your story, but don't forget you were sober on Monday morning.

BERT. Are you insinuating that I drink during the show ?

LILY. Insinuating ! That's a laugh. I'm not insinuating, I'm stating a fact. I can smell it a mile off. (*Crossing to her clothes-rack.*)

BERT. What a lady ! And what an artist, too—I don't suppose !

GEORGE (*crosses to* BENTLEY). Don't you talk in that tone to my wife.

LILY. Send for the manager, George. Send for Mr. Edwards.

BERT. I'm the one that's going to send for Mr. Edwards——

GEORGE. Get out of here before I crack you one——

(ALF *knocks at the door.*)

LILY. Come in !

(ALF *pushes open the door with his foot and comes in carry-ing a tray on which are two plates of steak and chips with other plates over them to keep them hot, a bottle of Al sauce and three bottles of Guinness.*)

ALF. You're wanted, Mr. Bentley, the sketch is nearly over.

BERT (*grimly, to the* PEPPERS). I'll be seeing you later.

(He goes out.)

GEORGE (*shouts after him*). Lounge lizard! Lousy son of a——

LILY (*to* ALF). Here, put it down on the hamper.

ALF (*doing so*). I've got the Player's in me pocket.

LILY (*feeling for them*). All right.

GEORGE. Come back later for the tray.

ALF. Righto.

(He goes out.)

GEORGE. Mr. Edwards—I'll have something to say to Mr. Edwards.

LILY. Lucky to play this date, are we? We'll see about that.

GEORGE. You were right, old girl.

LILY. What about—him?

GEORGE. Yes—dirty little rat.

LILY (*dragging up two chairs to the hamper*). Well, we all make mistakes sometimes—open the Guinness, there's a dear——

GEORGE. He's a little man, that's his trouble, never trust a man with short legs—brains too near their bottoms.

LILY. Come and sit down.

GEORGE (*opening a bottle of Guinness*). 'Alf a mo'——

LILY. That exit was too quick, you know!

GEORGE. All right—all right——

(They both sit down and begin to eat.)

They've forgotten the salt again——

LILY. No, here it is in a bit of paper——
GEORGE. Well, thank God for that, anyway——

(*The lights fade on the scene.*)

(*When the lights come up on the scene,* GEORGE *and* LILY *are sitting at their dressing-places freshening their make-ups. They both have a glass of Guinness within reach, and they are both wearing the rather frowsy dressing-gowns that they had put on during the preceding scene. The tray, with the remains of their dinner on it, is on the floor beside the hamper.*

GEORGE *gets up, opens the door and listens.*)

LILY. What's on ?

GEORGE. The Five Farthings.

LILY. That's the end of the first half—we'd better get a move on——

GEORGE (*returning to his place*). Fancy putting an act like that on at the end of the first half—you'd think they'd know better, wouldn't you ?

LILY. I wouldn't think they'd know better about anything in this hole.

GEORGE. It's a badly run house and it always has been.

(*He proceeds to put on his dress shirt, collar and tie, which are all in one with a zipper up the back.* LILY *is doing the same on her side of the room. They stuff wads of Kleenex paper in between their collars and their necks to prevent the make-up soiling their ties.*

There is a knock at the door.)

LILY. Who is it ?

MR. EDWARDS (*outside*). Mr. Edwards.

LILY (*pulling on her trousers*). Just a minute——

GEORGE (*under his breath*). Go easy—Bert Bentley's been at him.

LILY. I'll have something to say about that.

GEORGE. You leave it to me—I'll do the talking.

LILY. That'll be nice—— Come in.

(MR. EDWARDS *enters. He is the house manager and **very** resplendent. He is smoking a large cigar.*)

GEORGE (*rising and offering him a chair*).   Good evening, Mr. Edwards.

MR. EDWARDS (*disdaining it*).   Good evening.

LILY (*amially*).   How's the house ?

MR. EDWARDS.   Same as usual—full.

GEORGE.   That's fine, isn't it ?

LILY.   Do you want to sit down, Mr. Edwards ; we've been having a bit of a snack.

MR. EDWARDS (*grimly*).   I watched your act to-night, first house.

GEORGE (*gaily*).   There you are, Lil, what did I tell you—I had a sort of hunch you was out there—I said to my wife—what's the betting Mr. Edwards is out front ?—you know—you have a sort of feeling——

LILY.   Went well, didn't it ?

MR. EDWARDS.   I've seen things go better.

GEORGE.   We follow Betley Delavine, you know—a ballad singer—they always take a bit of warming up after a ballad singer.

LILY.   I'd defy Billy Bennet to get away with it in our place on the bill—I'd defy him—see ?

MR. EDWARDS.   There isn't anything wrong with your place on the bill.

GEORGE.   Well, I'd be willing to make a little bet with you—put the Five Farthings on before us and change Betley Delavine to the end of the first half and see what happens !

LILY.   You'd send them out to the bars and they'd stay there.

MR. EDWARDS.   I did not come here to discuss the running of my theatre.

GEORGE.   Oh—sorry, I'm sure.

MR. EDWARDS.   That exit of yours killed the whole act.

GEORGE.   A little mishap—anybody might drop a telescope——

LILY.   Even a sailor.

MR. EDWARDS.   It looked terrible.

GEORGE.   The tempo was all wrong, Mr. Edwards.

MR. EDWARDS.   Sounded all right to me.

GEORGE. Maybe it did, but we know our own numbers, you know.

MR. EDWARDS. It didn't look like it from the front.

GEORGE. We've never had any trouble before—that exit's stopped the show in every town we've played.

LILY. A musical director can make or mar an act, you know—make or mar it.

MR. EDWARDS. Mr. Bentley is one of the finest musical directors in the business.

LILY. Then he's wasted here, that's all I can say.

GEORGE (*warningly*). Lily!

LILY. Well, if he's so wonderful, why isn't he at the Albert Hall—doing Hiawatha ——

MR. EDWARDS. I understand you had words with Mr. Bentley.

GEORGE. We did, and we will again if he starts any of his funny business.

MR. EDWARDS. I understand that you accused him of drinking during the show.

LILY. Getting quite bright, aren't you?

GOERGE. Shut up, Lil; leave this to me.

MR. EDWARDS. Did you or did you not?

GEORGE. Look here, who d'you think you are—coming talking to us like this?

MR. EDWARDS. Did you or did you not accuse Mr. Bentley of drinking during the show?

LILY (*heatedly*). Yes, we did, because he does, so there!

MR. EDWARDS. That's serious, you know—it's slander.

LILY. I don't care if it's arson, it's true!

MR. EDWARDS. Now look here, Mrs. Pepper, I think it only fair to warn you——

LILY (*rises*). And I think it's only fair to warn you that unless you get a better staff in this theatre and a better orchestra and a better musical director, you'll find yourself a cinema inside six months!

MR. EDWARDS. You won't gain anything by losing your temper.

GEORGE. And you won't gain anything by coming

round back-stage and throwing your weight about—
your place is in the front of the house—My theatre this
and My theatre that—it's no more your theatre than
what it is ours—you're on a salary same as us, and I'll
bet it's a damn sight less, too, and don't you forget it——

MR. EDWARDS (*losing his temper*). I'm not going to
stand any more of this——

LILY. Oh, put it where the monkey put the nuts!

MR. EDWARDS. I'll guarantee one thing, anyhow,
you'll never play this date again as long as I'm in
charge——

GEORGE. In charge of what, the Fire Brigade!

LILY. Play this date—anybody'd think it was the
Palladium to hear you talk——

GEORGE. You'd better be careful, Mr. Edwards—
you don't want a scandal like this to get round the
profession——

MR. EDWARDS. What are you talking about?

GEORGE. I'm talking about the way this house is
run.

MR. EDWARDS (*working up*). You mind your own
business!

LILY. More than one act's been mucked up here,
you know, by that orchestra of yours—it's beginning to
get a name——

MR. EDWARDS. Oh, it is, is it?

GEORGE. They're all over the shop—no discipline.

LILY. What can you expect with a drunk in charge
of it!

MR. EDWARDS (*raising his voice*). Look here—you
stop talking like that or it'll be the worse for you.

GEORGE. His tempos are wrong and he hasn't got
any authority over his men——

LILY. This date's only a fill in for us, you know——

GEORGE. You ask our agents.

MR. EDWARDS. I shall report this conversation.

LILY. Do—report it to the Lord Mayor—if you're
sober enough to remember the lyrics. (*She goes up
stage.*)

GEORGE. Shut up, Lil.

MR. EDWARDS. I will not stay here and argue——
GEORGE. You're dead right, you won't——

MR. EDWARDS (*tapping him on the shoulder*). You were a flop last time you played here and you've been a flop this time, and that's enough for me——

LILY (*screaming—tapping him on the shoulder*). Flop ! What d'you mean, flop ! We're a bigger draw than anybody on the bill——

(*There is a knock on the door.*)

GEORGE (*loudly*). Come in——

(MISS MABEL GRACE *enters. She is a faded ex-West End actress wearing a towel round her head to keep her hair in place, and an elaborate dressing-gown.*)

MABEL GRACE (*acidly*). Good evening—I'm sorry to intrude—but you're making such a dreadful noise I'm quite unable to rest——

MR. EDWARDS. I'm very sorry, Miss Grace——

MABEL GRACE. I find it hard enough to play a big emotional scene twice a night in any case——

LILY. Oh, that's an emotional scene, is it ? I wondered what it was——

MABEL GRACE. I am not accustomed to being spoken to in that tone, Mrs. Whatever-your-name-is——

LILY. Pepper's the name—Pepper—P-E-P-P-E-R—same as what you put in your soup.

MABEL GRACE (*coldly*). Very interesting.

MR. EDWARDS. I apologize, Miss Grace.

MABEL GRACE (*grandly*). Thank you, Mr. Edwards.

GEORGE (*in an affected voice*). What you must think of us, Miss Grace—so common—we're mortified, we are really—and you fresh from His Majesty's.

LILY. Fairly fresh.

MABEL GRACE. Mr. Edwards, I'm really not used to dressing-room brawls—I'll leave it to you to see that there is no further noise——

LILY. Except for the raspberries at the end of your sketch—even Mr. God Almighty Edwards can't control those——

MABEL GRACE. You're almost as vulgar off the stage as you are on, I congratulate you.

LILY (*very loudly*). Vulgar, are we! (*She crosses to* MABEL GRACE.) I'd like to ask you something. If you're so bloody West End, why the hell did you leave it?

GEORGE. There'll be an answer to that in next Sunday's edition.

LILY. Thank you, George.

(*They shake hands.*)

MR. EDWARDS. Look here, you two, I've had about enough of this——

GEORGE. You've had about enough, have you? What about us?——

(*The conversation becomes simultaneous.*)

LILY. You and your big cigar and your white waistcoat and your Woolworth studs! Alfred Butt with knobs on——

GEORGE. You get out of here, you fat fool, before I throw you out!——

MABEL GRACE. Thank you for your courtesy, Mr. Edwards——

MR. EDWARDS. I'll see you don't play this date any more or any other date, either——

LILY. Play this date again—thank you for the rabbit—I'd sooner play Ryde Pier in November——

(*In the middle of the pandemonium* ALF *puts his head round the door.*)

ALF (*yelling*). Red Peppers—three minutes——
GEORGE. Good God! We're off——
LILY (*wildly*). Get out, all of you—get out——

(GEORGE *takes* MR. EDWARDS *by the shoulders and shoves him out of the room.* MABEL GRACE, *laughing affectedly, follows him.*

LILY *and* GEORGE *put on their wigs, powder their make-ups, tweak their ties into place, grab their hats and canes—then, muttering curses under their breaths, they*

*collect their sailor clothes and sailor wigs and telescopes
and rush out of the room as the lights fade.)*

The lights come up on the CURTAIN *as the orchestra is
playing their introduction music. The* CURTAIN *rises
on the street scene again. They make their entrance for
the " dude " number, " Men About Town."*

Routine.

DUDE NUMBER : " MEN ABOUT TOWN."

Verse.

BOTH. We're two chaps who
Find it thrilling
To do the killing,
We're always willing
To give the girls a treat.
Just a drink at the Ritz,
Call it double or quits,
Then we feel the world is at our feet.
Top hats, white spats
Look divine on us,
There's a shine on us,
Get a line on us
When we come your way.
Gad ! eleven o'clock !
Let's pop into the Troc.
Ere we start the business of the day.

Refrain 1.

As we stroll down Picc—Piccadilly,
In the bright morning air,
All the girls turn and stare,
We're so nonchalant and frightfully debonair ;
When we chat to Rose, Maud or Lily,
You should see the way their boy friends frown,
For they know without a doubt
That their luck's right out
Up against a couple of men about town.

Refrain 2.

As we stroll down Picc—Piccadilly,
All the girls say, " Who's here ?
Put your hat straight, my dear,
For it's Marmaduke and Percy Vere de Vere."
As we doff hats, each pretty filly,
Gives a wink at us and then looks down,
For they long with all their might
For a red-hot night
When they see a couple of men about town.

*(They then do a rather complicated tap dance, towards the
end of which* BERT BENTLEY *quickens the time so that
*LILY *barges into* GEORGE, *knocking him over into the
footlights.* LILY *calls for " Curtain " and the* CURTAIN
falls. They exit through the centre of it.)

PROPERTY PLOT

As used at the Phœnix Theatre

1. Old wooden table with 2 make-up towels, 1 towel spread on table, grease-paints, broken cigar-box, Kleenex papers, hand-mirror, tin of grease with lid off, box of matches, 20 packet of Player's with 2 cigarettes, glass of water, powder and puff.

2. Old long wooden table with 2 huckaback towels, 1 towel spread on table, grease-paints, tin of grease, Kleenex papers, glass bowl of hairpins, brush and comb, hare's foot, nail-polisher, powder and puff in bowl, hand-mirror, laundry bills.

3. Old travelling-basket labelled "Red Peppers."

4. Sink in stand with tube and pail, towel, soap, nailbrush, warm water.

5, 6, 7, 8. Bentwood chairs.

Notices on walls, "No Smoking," etc.

Large mirror over each table.

Board for letters hung on backing, R.

Off stage R.—2 telescopes, 2 walking-sticks.

9. Clothes-rack and 2 curtain boards with coat (containing silver coins in pocket) vest, trousers, coat-hangers, dressing-gown, hat, macintosh, shoes, shirt, collar, drawers.

10. Curtain board and clothes-rack with clothes-hangers, 2 dressing-gowns, dress, ladies' underclothes, stockings, hat, coat, shoes. Various boxes on top of board.

Off stage R.

Packet of 20 Player's cigarettes.

Cigar.

Tray with 2 plates of chips and gingerbread—two plates cover these—screw of salt, 2 screw-top Guinness, 2 glasses, 2 knives and forks, tray-cloth, bottle of sauce.

SCENE 2

Fold tray-cloth over tray.

Put chairs back.

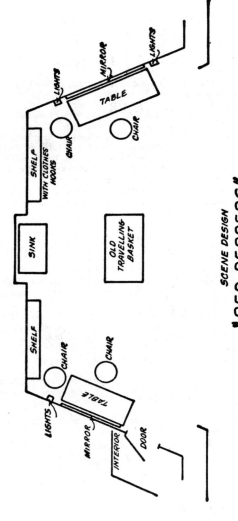

SCENE DESIGN

"RED PEPPERS"

HOME-BUILT
Lighting Equipment
for The Small Stage
By THEODORE FUCHS

This volume presents a series of fourteen simplified designs for building various types of stage lighting and control equipment, with but one purpose in mind—to enable the amateur producer to acquire a complete set of stage lighting equipment at the lowest possible cost. The volume is 8½" x 11" in size, with heavy paper and spiral binding—features which make the volume well suited to practical workshop use.

Community Theatre
A MANUAL FOR SUCCESS
By JOHN WRAY YOUNG

The ideal text for anyone interested in participating in Community Theatre as a vocation or avocation. "Organizing a Community Theatre," "A Flight Plan for the Early Years," "Programming for People—Not Computers," and other chapters are blueprints for solid growth. "Technical, Business and Legal Procedures" cuts a safe and solvent path through some tricky undergrowth. Essential to the library of all community theatres, and to the schools who will supply them with talent in the years to come.

Other Publications for Your Interest

MOVIE OF THE MONTH
(COMEDY)
By DANIEL MELTZER

2 men—Interior

This new comedy by the author of the ever-popular *The Square Root of Love* is an amusing satire of commercial television. B.S., a TV programming executive, is anxious to bolster his network's ratings, which have been sagging of late due to programming disasters such as a documentary called "The Ugly Truth" (says B.S.: "What the hell is The Ugly Truth, and how the hell did it get into our Prime Time?") His eagerbeaver assistant, appropriately named Broun, has found a script which he is sure can be made into a hit "Movie of the Month". It's about this Danish prince, see, who comes home from college to find that his uncle has murdered his father and married his mother . . . Well, naturally, B.S. has his own ideas about how to fix such a totally unbelievable plot . . .   (#17621)

SUNDANCE
(ALL GROUPS—COMEDY)
By MEIR Z. RIBALOW

5 men—Simple interior

This new comedy from the author of *Shrunken Heads* is set in a sort of metaphysical wild west saloon. The characters include Hickock, Jesse, the Kid, and the inevitable Barkeep. Hickock kills to uphold the law. Jesse kills for pleasure. The Kid kills to bring down The Establishment. What if, wonders the Barkeep, they met up with the Ultimate Killer—who kills for no reason, who kills simply because that's what he does? Enter Sundance. He does not kill to uphold the law, for pleasure, or to make a political statement, or because he had a deprived childhood. And he proceeds to kill everyone, exiting at the end with his sixguns blazing! "Witty, strong, precise, unusually well-written."—The Guardian. "A brilliant piece."—Dublin Evening Press. This co-winner of the 1981 Annual NYC Metropolitan Short Play Festival has been a success in 6 countries!   (#3113)